African Elephants

by Roland Smith
photographs by Gerry Ellis

 Lerner Publications Company • Minneapolis, Minnesota

For Thandi and Moyo—two African elephants I had the pleasure of watching grow up.

—RS

To Bug, who is smaller than an elephant but with a heart and spirit just as large.

—GE

Thanks to our series consultant, Sharyn Fenwick, elementary science/math specialist. Mrs. Fenwick was the winner of the National Science Teachers Association 1991 Distinguished Teaching Award. She also was the recipient of the Presidential Award for Excellence in Math and Science Teaching, representing the state of Minnesota at the elementary level in 1992.

I want to thank Ruth Berman for her astute editing, and her wonderful guidance in helping me to write this book.

—RS

Ruth Berman, series editor
Steve Foley, series designer

Library of Congress Cataloging-in-Publication Data

Smith, Roland, 1951–
    African elephants / by Roland Smith ; photos by Gerry Ellis.
        p. cm.— (Early bird nature books)
    Includes index.
    ISBN 0-8225-3006-6
    1. African elephant—Juvenile literature. [1. African elephant.
2. Elephants.] I. Ellis, Gerry. ill. II. Title. III. Series.
QL737.P98S65 1995
599.6'1096—dc20   94-34313

Manufactured in the United States of America
1 2 3 4 5 6 – I/SP – 00 99 98 97 96 95

Contents

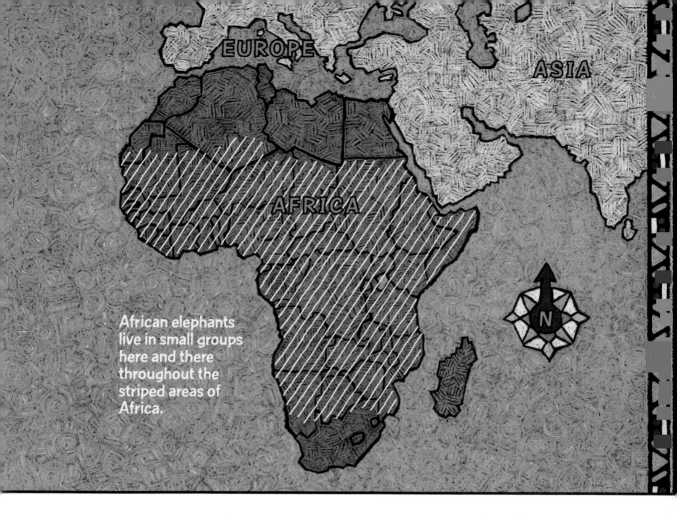

African elephants live in small groups here and there throughout the striped areas of Africa.

Be a Word Detective

Can you find these words as you read about the African elephant's life? Be a detective and try to figure out what they mean. You can turn to the glossary on page 46 for help.

bulls	habitat	nomads
calf	herbivores	nurse
cows	herds	pachyderms
extinct	matriarch	predators

Chapter 1

There are two kinds of elephants, African and Asian. This book is about African elephants. How tall do you think they can grow?

The Biggest Animal on Land

There is nothing quite like an elephant. Elephants have wrinkled gray skin and floppy ears. Two huge teeth called tusks grow out of

6

their mouths. And they have long, strange-looking noses called trunks. The African elephant is the largest animal on land. An adult male African elephant stands 11 feet tall at the shoulder. He can weigh more than a school bus.

The scientific name of African elephants is Loxodonta africana. They can weigh up to 15,000 pounds.

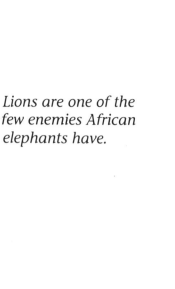

Lions are one of the few enemies African elephants have.

Elephants are so big that they don't have many enemies. Besides people, the elephant's main enemy is the lion. Lions are predators (PRED-uh-turz). They kill other animals for food. Most elephants are even too big for a lion. But from time to time, lions *will* try to kill young elephants.

African elephants have huge ears. They can be over 6 feet long from top to bottom. Elephants flap their ears to cool themselves on hot days. They also stretch their ears out when they're angry or frightened. By stretching their ears, elephants look even bigger than they actually are. This helps to scare enemies away.

The ears of African elephants are shaped like the country they come from.

Elephants are sometimes called pachyderms (PAK-uh-durms). Pachyderm means thick-skinned. An elephant's skin is 1 inch thick and very tough. Thick skin protects elephants from being hurt by sharp thorns and branches. The rhinoceros and hippopotamus are pachyderms too.

Very little hair grows out of the elephant's thick skin. Even though the skin on this elephant's tail looks tough, elephant skin is soft to the touch.

Dust helps protect the elephant's sensitive skin.

Even with thick skin, elephants are bothered by insect bites and sunburn. So they roll in mud. They also use their trunks to blow dust over their bodies. Mud and dust protect elephants from insects and the sun.

Chapter 2

The trunk is a combination of the nose and the upper lip. How many muscles do you think there are in a trunk?

Terrific Trunks

Elephants use their trunks for smelling, breathing, eating, and digging. And elephants are the only animals on earth that can pick up things with their noses! Elephants use their powerful trunks like we use our arms. An elephant's trunk has over 60,000 muscles! We have only a little more than 600 muscles in our whole body. With their trunks, elephants can pull up trees. And they can reach food way above their heads.

Elephants use their trunks to greet each other. It's their way of saying hello.

At the end of the trunk are two nubs. The nubs act like fingers. Elephants use these fingers to pick up objects. They can even pick up something as small as a dime.

Elephants can use the nubs at the end of their trunks to pick up small objects.

Elephants make special deep sounds that are so low people can't hear them. But elephants can hear these low sounds as far as 6 miles away.

Elephants also use their trunks to help make many different sounds. When they are frightened or angry, elephants make a loud trumpeting sound. When they are happy or excited, they make high, squeaky sounds.

Elephants cool down in a swamp.

Elephants love the water. They take baths
to stay cool. When they are under water,
elephants can breathe by sticking their trunks

Young elephants rest after taking a mud bath.

above the water's surface. Elephants also take showers to stay cool. They use their trunks to blow water over their backs.

Chapter 3

Elephants actually walk on their toes. They walk long distances every day. Why do you think they have to walk so far?

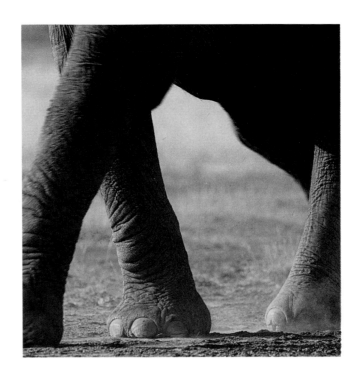

Eating and Drinking

Elephants are nomads. They must keep wandering through Africa, looking for food and water. They have no fixed homes. Elephants eat over 300 pounds of food a day. To find this much food to eat, elephants sometimes have to travel dozens of miles a day.

If elephants stayed in one spot, there would be nothing left for them to eat. Adult elephants usually march along at 6 miles per hour. But they can run up to 25 miles per hour for short distances.

Elephants are herbivores (HUR-buh-vorz). They eat only plants. They use their trunks to pull up clumps of grass, pick fruits and vegetables, and strip leaves and bark from trees. Then they stuff the food into their mouths. Sometimes the

Elephants wrap their powerful trunks around branches to get their food.

After picking its food, an elephant uses its trunk like you would use a fork or spoon.

food in a tree is too high for elephants to reach. Then they pound the tree with their foreheads until the food drops to the ground. If this doesn't work, elephants use their great strength to try to pull up the tree. Or, they try to push the tree over so they can reach the food.

A thirsty elephant sucks up a trunkful of water.

A wild elephant drinks 40 gallons of water a day. That's more than enough water to fill a garbage can. Elephants suck water into their trunks. Then they blow the water into their mouths. A thirsty elephant can suck up many gallons of water at a time. Elephants often stay near rivers and springs because they need so much water.

After an elephant has a trunkful of water, it squirts the water into its mouth.

A baby elephant stands at the edge of a waterhole.

When there is no water, elephants use their tusks, feet, and trunks to dig for water. They make holes that may be filled with water for some time. Other African animals, like lions, zebras, and baboons, drink the water from these holes too.

A male African elephant's tusk can grow as long as 11½ feet and weigh as much as 235 pounds.

Both male and female African elephants grow tusks. Tusks are actually teeth growing outside of the elephant's mouth. Tusks grow throughout the elephant's life. Elephants keep their tusks worn down by using them to dig in the ground and to strip bark off of trees.

Elephants also have four large teeth made for grinding food. As these teeth wear down, new teeth push the old teeth out. During their lives, elephants go through six sets of grinding teeth.

This elephant is using the grinding teeth inside its mouth to chew its food.

Chapter 4

This group of elephants made up of mothers and youngsters is called a herd. How many elephants do you think are usually in a herd?

Elephant Herds

Elephants travel together in groups called herds. A herd has about 12 to 20 elephants in it. Sometimes, many herds come together, making a giant herd of hundreds of elephants.

A matriarch leads her herd to food and water.

An elephant herd is made up of females and their youngsters. Female elephants are called cows. The biggest and oldest cow is the leader of the herd. She is called the matriarch (MAY-tree-ark).

The matriarch leads the herd to food and water. She also guides the elephants to areas where they can sleep. Elephants sleep standing on their feet or lying down. The herd stops and rests for a few hours every day and night. The best places to rest are under shady trees or next to rivers and lakes.

A herd of elephants eats and rests.

Male elephants are called bulls. Bulls leave the herd when they are about 10 years old. They live alone or in herds with other bulls. These male groups are called bachelor (BACH-lur) herds.

Bull elephants live alone or in bachelor herds.

Chapter 5

*Baby elephants have
a lot of fuzzy hair.
How big do you think
a baby elephant is
when it is born?*

Baby Elephants

A female elephant gives birth to a baby elephant about once every five years. A baby elephant is called a calf. When an elephant is born, it weighs a little over 200 pounds. And it's about 3 feet tall. A half hour after it's born,

Calves are able to walk with the herd very soon after they're born.

the calf can stand up. If a calf has trouble getting to its feet, its mother lifts up the calf with her trunk. Within a couple of days, the calf is strong enough to move with the herd.

Calves nurse, or drink their mother's milk, right after they stand up for the first time. They start eating solid food, like grasses, when they are a few months old. But calves continue nursing for at least two years.

Calves use their mouths, not their trunks, to nurse.

The whole elephant herd helps take care of the calf. The elephants use their bodies to shade the calf from the hot sun. Sometimes a mother and calf can't keep up with the herd. Then a few herd members stay behind. They help protect mother and calf by chasing predators away.

A mother elephant shades her calf from the hot sun.

Left: *A mother and an older brother or sister take care of a newborn calf.*

Below: *All the elephants in a herd help take care of the calves.*

Chapter 6

Elephants can live to be 60 years old. A mother elephant has a new calf every five years or so. Do you think African elephants live everywhere in Africa?

Elephants in Danger

Elephants were once found in great numbers. They lived all through Africa, from the cool, high mountains to the hot, flat grasslands.

Sadly, there aren't as many elephants as there used to be. The African elephant is now found only in a few small areas of central and eastern Africa. Some scientists think that the African elephant will be extinct in the wild within the next few years. When an animal is extinct, it's gone forever.

Many elephants are dying because there isn't enough for them to eat. This elephant has been dead for a long time.

In most African countries, it's against the law to kill elephants. But some people kill elephants anyway. People who break laws to kill animals are called poachers. Poachers kill elephants for their tusks. Elephant tusks are made out of ivory. Ivory can be sold for a lot of money. An elephant tusk weighing a hundred pounds can sell for nearly $5,000.

Tusks were used to decorate this gong.

The government took all these tusks away from poachers.

The United States and many other countries are trying to save the elephants. They've made it against the law to buy ivory. If people stop buying ivory, then maybe poachers will stop killing elephants.

This young elephant may have a hard time finding food.

Another reason there are so few elephants
is that their habitat is being destroyed. Habitat
is everything that makes up an animal's home.
The food it eats, the water it drinks, and the
land it lives on all make up an animal's habitat.

In Africa, people have built farms on much of the elephant's habitat. These farms have pushed elephant herds into small areas. There isn't enough for the elephants to eat. So herds of

An elephant herd walks in search of food.

elephants raid the farms for food. They destroy farmers' crops. Sometimes, the government has to kill the elephants to stop them. To help save elephants, many African governments have set up parks where elephants can live in peace.

Some scientists are afraid that elephants will soon be extinct. So there are parks where elephants can live peacefully.

Trunks, tails, ears, skin, and tusks make the elephant like no other animal on earth.

There is no other animal like the elephant. For thousands of years, these gray, gentle giants have wandered through Africa. Now, few elephants live in the wild. We can help save the elephant if we protect its home and stop buying ivory. The elephant's survival depends on us.

On Sharing a Book

As you know, adults greatly influence a child's attitude toward reading. When a child sees you read, or when you share a book with a child, you're sending a message that reading is important. Show your child that reading a book together is important to you. Find a comfortable, quiet place. Turn off the television and limit other distractions like telephone calls.

Be prepared to start slowly. Take turns reading parts of this book. Stop and talk about what you're reading. Talk about the photographs. You may find that much of the shared time is spent discussing just a few pages. This discussion time is valuable for both of you, so don't move through the book too quickly. If your child begins to lose interest, stop reading. Continue sharing the book at another time. When you do pick up the book again, be sure to revisit the parts you have already read. Most importantly, enjoy the book!

Be a Vocabulary Detective

You will find a word list on page 5. Words selected for this list are important to the understanding of the topic of this book. Encourage your child to be a word detective and search for the words as you read the book together. Talk about what the words mean and how they are used in the sentence. Do any of these words have more than one meaning? You will find these words defined in a glossary on page 46.

What about Questions?

Use questions to make sure your child understands the information in this book. Here are some suggestions:

> What did this paragraph tell us? What does this picture show? What do you think we'll learn about next? Could an elephant live in your backyard? Why/Why not? What would you need to live where elephants live? How do elephants protect themselves from the sun? How does an elephant use its trunk? How is an elephant herd like your family and how is it different? What do you think it's like being an elephant? What if there were no elephants? What is your favorite part of the book? Why?

If your child has questions, don't hesitate to respond with questions of your own like: What do *you* think? Why? What is it that you don't know? If your child can't remember certain facts, turn to the index.

Introducing the Index

The index is an important learning tool. It helps readers get information quickly without searching throughout the whole book. Turn to the index on page 47. Choose an entry, such as *trunk*, and ask your child to use the index to find out how elephants use their trunks. Repeat this exercise with as many entries as you like. Ask your child to point out the differences between an index and a glossary. (The glossary tells readers what words mean, while the index helps readers find information quickly.)

Where in the World?

Many plants and animals found in the Early Bird Nature Books series live in parts of the world other than the United States. Encourage your child to find the places mentioned in this book on a world map or globe. Take time to talk about climate, terrain, and how your family might live in such places.

All the World in Metric!

Although our monetary system is in metric units (based on multiples of 10), the United States is one of the few countries in the world that does not use the metric system of measurement. Here are some conversion activities you and your child can do using a calculator:

WHEN YOU KNOW:	MULTIPLY BY:	TO FIND:
miles	1.609	kilometers
feet	0.3048	meters
inches	2.54	centimeters
gallons	3.787	liters
tons	0.907	metric tons
pounds	0.454	kilograms

Family Activities

Have your child make up a story about elephants. Be sure information from this book is included. Have your child illustrate the story.

Visit a zoo to see elephants. Are they African or Asian elephants? What are the physical differences between African and Asian elephants? How are they similar to other pachyderms at the zoo and how are they different?

Act out being elephants. What happens when an enemy is near? How do you get food and water? What do you do when heat or insects bother you?

Glossary

bulls—male elephants

calf—a baby elephant

cows—female elephants

extinct—a whole group of animals that is not living anymore

habitat—the place where an animal lives and grows

herbivores (HUR-buh-vorz)—animals who eat only plants

herds—groups of animals that live together

matriarch (MAY-tree-ark)—a female leader

nomads—animals who wander from place to place

nurse—to drink mother's milk

pachyderms (PAK-uh-durms)—animals with thick skin

predators (PRED-uh-turz)—animals who hunt and eat other animals

Index

Pages listed in **bold** type refer to photographs.

About the Author

Roland Smith has worked with elephants—both Asian and African—for over 20 years. In his career, he has been a zoo keeper, senior zoo keeper, curator of mammals and birds, general curator, assistant zoo director, and senior research biologist. Roland has appeared on several local and national television shows, including the National Geographic special called *Elephants.* He has written other books for children, including *Sea Otter Rescue, Inside the Zoo Nursery,* and *Thunder Cave.* He is the author of *Vultures,* another title in Lerner's Early Bird Nature Books series. Roland and his wife, Marie, live on a small farm in Stafford, Oregon.

About the Photographer

Gerry Ellis has explored the world as a professional photographer and naturalist for over two decades. From his home base in Portland, Oregon, he has traveled to remote areas of Africa in search of elephants. Gerry's images of the rarest and most beautiful of the earth's wilds have garnered numerous accolades, including multiple awards in the prestigious BBC Wildlife Photographer of the Year competition. His work is continually featured in *Ranger Rick, National Geographic World, Terre Savage, TIME,* and *Smithsonian.* It has also been featured in the books *Safari, The Outdoor Traveler's Guide to Australia, Gorillas,* and *America's Rainforest.* Gerry's current projects include books for Lerner on mountain gorillas, chimpanzees, and orangutans.